◆FOCUS◆
Reading for Success

Sing and Dance

PROGRAM AUTHORS
Richard L. Allington
Ronald L. Cramer
Patricia M. Cunningham
G. Yvonne Pérez
Constance Frazier Robinson
Robert J. Tierney

PROGRAM CONSULTANTS
Bernadine J. Bolden
Ann Hall
Sylvia M. Lee
Dolores Perez
Jo Ann Wong

CRITIC READERS
Shirley Duncan
Helen Johncock
Eunice Shepard
Joy Stewart

John C. Manning, *Instructional Consultant*

SCOTT, FORESMAN AND COMPANY
Editorial Offices: Glenview, Illinois

Regional Offices: Sunnyvale, California •
Tucker, Georgia • Glenview, Illinois •
Oakland, New Jersey • Dallas, Texas

ACKNOWLEDGMENTS

Text

First four stanzas from "Apple Blossoms" by Ralph Bergengren from *Jane, Joseph and John* by Ralph Bergengren. Copyright 1918 by Atlantic Monthly Press, Inc. Copyright renewed 1946 by Ralph Bergengren. Reprinted by permission of Atlantic-Little, Brown.

"Foal" by Mary Britton Miller. Reprinted by permission of the Estate of Mary Britton Miller.

"Jewels Floating By" (Text only) from *Up and Down the River* by Claudia Lewis. Copyright © 1979 by Claudia Lewis. Reprinted by permission of Harper & Row, Publishers, Inc., McIntosh and Otis, Inc. and the author.

"Lewis Has a Trumpet" (Text only) from *Dogs & Dragons, Trees & Dreams* by Karla Kuskin. Copyright © 1958 by Karla Kuskin. Reprinted by permission of Harper & Row, Publishers, Inc.

"Pet Show" by Arthur Guiterman. Adapted by permission of Louise H. Sclove.

"Tommy" in *Bronzeville Boys and Girls* by Gwendolyn Brooks. Copyright © 1956 by Gwendolyn Brooks Blakely. Reprinted by permission of Harper & Row, Publishers, Inc.

Stories by: Ruth Kaye, Liane Onish, Sallie Runck, Nancy Ross Ryan, Mary Shuter

Photographs

Page 64: Grant Heilman;   Page 95: Dennis Kucharzak; Pages 122–123: Craig Aurness/West Light;   Pages 148–149, 157: Carl Roessler/CLICK/Chicago;   Pages 155, 158: Photo courtesy The Cousteau Society, 930 W. 21st St., Norfolk, VA 23517, a membership-supported environmental organization;   Page 156: Jeff Rotman/Peter Arnold, Inc.; Pages 170–171: John Running/Photo Library;   Page 172 (right): Wide World Photos;   Page 173: The National Archives;   Pages 172 (left), 174: Courtesy Explorers Club Archives;   Page 175: By Admiral Robert E. Peary. Courtesy Edward P. Stafford. © National Geographic Society;   Pages 176, 178–179: L & M Photos/FPG

Artists

Allen, David 112–117;   Brewster, Patience 166–169;   Cheng, Judith 103–109;   Eberbach, Andrea 78–81, 83, 100–101;   Engelbreit, Mary 133;   Esposito, Vivian 68–76;   Frazee, Marla 136–138, 140–142, 144–146, 188–191;   Kock, Carl 28, 66–67, 110, 182–183, 214;   Lanza, Barbara 150–154, 194–204;   Loccisano, Karen 162–165;   McIntosh, Jon 45–49;   Mitchell, Kurt 8–27, 30–32, 34–37, 39–42;   Musgrave, Steve 193;   Randstrom, Susan 84–87;   Rigie, Jane 160–161, 207–213;   Rosenheim, Cindy 7, 43, 77, 90–91, 93–94, 111, 147, 181;   Roth, Gail 112–114, 116–117;   Sanford, John 180;   Wilson, Ann 54–61, 63;   Wilson, Don 88–89, 215–221

Freelance Photographs

Jim Ballard 52, 118–121, 124–128, 130–131, 184–187; Ryan Roessler 50, 53, 159, 205–206

Cover Artist

Steve Musgrave

ISBN 0-673-72007-1

Contents

Section One

Sunshine and Flowers

Groundhogs Like Spring

In the spring, the farmer puts seeds
and little plants in the ground.
Rain and sun will help them grow.

The House in the Ground

Millie the groundhog lives here.
She lives with Grandpa Groundhog.
They live in a house in the ground.

One day Millie was reading a book.
Something went drip, drip, drip.

"What is dripping on my head?"
asked Millie the groundhog.

Grandpa said, "I don't know.
Let's see why it is wet in here."

The two went up to look around.

Grandpa said, "See, it is raining. And here is a hole in the house. It rains in the hole, and so it gets wet in the house. I will have to work on that hole."

"Now I see why the rain makes it wet in the house," Millie said.

She looked away and asked, "Who is that?"

"That is a farmer," said Grandpa.

"What is she doing?" asked Millie.

Grandpa said, "She is putting little
plants in the ground.
The rain will help her plants grow."

Then Millie said, "Let's go!
Here comes more rain!
I don't want to get wet!"

Millie the groundhog ran to
her house.
But her grandpa walked.

When Grandpa came in, he said, "You did not get wet."

Millie said, "No, but more water is dripping down that hole.
Drip, drip, drip.
This time I will not get wet.
I will keep my coat on!"

Seeds in the Ground

Millie the groundhog asked,
"Grandpa, is it a wet day?
Will the water drip in the hole?
Will it get wet in here?"

Grandpa said, "No, it is not wet.
The sun is out."

Taking her hat, Millie said, "Let's
go up to see if the farmer is out.
I want to see the farmer working."

"Let's go," said Grandpa.

They went up to look at the farmer.

"This is not the same farmer.
Why is this farmer putting seeds in
the ground?" asked Millie.

Grandpa said, "Plants will grow from
the seeds in the ground."

Millie looked at the ground.

She asked, "What is the farmer
growing?"

Grandpa said, "We will see.
But now I need to sleep."

Grandpa went to sleep.

Millie, the little groundhog, put on her hat.
She sat in the hot sun.
She looked at the ground where the farmer planted seeds.

She said, "Now I will see what plants grow out of the ground.
Grow, little seeds, grow."

After his nap, Grandpa talked.

He said, "Millie, let's go back now.
I must work on that hole in
the house."

Millie said, "But I want to see what
plants grow out of the ground."

Grandpa said, "It takes time for
plants to grow.
Let's go back to the house.
I will find some seeds for
you to plant."

Next to her house, Millie planted
some seeds the way the farmer did.

Work in the Field

The days are hot.
The sun is bright in the sky.
The plants grow in the field.

A Walk in the Field

The sun was bright in the sky.
Millie looked where she planted her
sunflower seeds.

Millie said, "Grandpa, look!
I have big sunflowers that look as
bright as the sun in the sky.
The farmers have plants, and so do I.
Did the farmers grow sunflowers too?"

Grandpa said, "No, they have corn.
You can go to the field and look.
But don't let the farmers see you."

Millie walked to the farmer's field.

Millie saw a bird in the sky.

The bird said, "Hello!
Come eat corn with me."

Millie said, "I don't want corn.
Soon I'll have sunflower
seeds to eat."

Just then, Millie saw the farmers.

She asked the bird, "What are the
farmers doing?"

The bird said, "One farmer is watering plants.
She has a shiny watering can.
The man has a long stick.
He is working in the ground around the corn."

Millie said, "I see something bright and shiny in the field.
Let's go see what it is."

They went to see the shiny thing.

Millie said, "It looks like a farmer.
She has a shiny hat on her head!
Her hair looks like straw."

The bird said, "Her hair **is** straw.
The farmers put her in the field to
scare birds away.
But she does not scare me."

Millie said, "She scares me!
I am going back to my house."

Just then, the farmer started to
shake his stick and chase them.
The bird went flying away into the sky.
Millie ran to her house in the ground.

Millie's Secret

Millie and Grandpa
sat down to talk.

She said, "The farmer
chased me.
He scared me.
Something in the field scared
me too."

Grandpa said, "The farmer does
not want animals to eat his corn.
He scares you and the
birds away."

Millie said, "Let's go see if the
farmers are eating my sunflowers.
I will scare the farmers away!"

Grandpa and Millie went to
her field.

They did not see any farmers.

Grandpa said, "You don't need to
scare the farmers away.
But you can water your sunflowers.
I made a new watering can for you."

Millie said, "Thank you, Grandpa.
Now my sunflowers will grow to
the sky!
If the farmers want my sunflowers, I
will scare them away."

Millie watered her sunflowers.

The next day, the sky was bright.
Grandpa worked in Millie's field.
He watered her sunflowers.

Then Grandpa saw something bright in
the sunflower field.
He saw a groundhog with long hair.
A shiny pan was on its head.

Grandpa went to look at it.

Millie said, "Grandpa, I made a
groundhog for my field.
Did she scare you?
Do you like her bright hair?
I made her hair out of straw.
No farmers will eat my seeds.
My groundhog will scare them away!"

Grandpa laughed at the groundhog.
He laughed at her straw hair.
Then he patted Millie on the back.

He said, "Your groundhog works.
I don't see any farmers!"

To be read by the teacher

Tommy

by Gwendolyn Brooks

I put a seed into the ground
And said, "I'll watch it grow."
I watered it and cared for it
As well as I could know.

One day I walked in my backyard,
And oh, what did I see!
My seed had popped itself right out,
Without consulting me.

Just for You

Make a puppet.

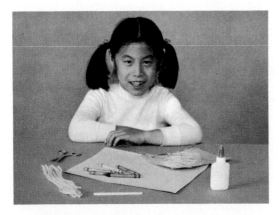

1. This is what you need.

2. Cut out your puppet.

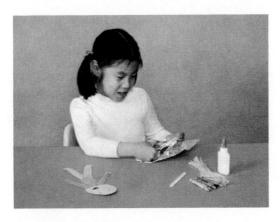

3. Cut some bright hair
   and a shiny hat.

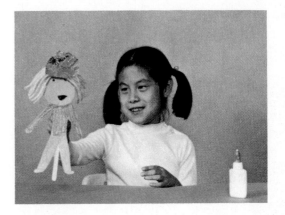

4. Paste your new
   puppet on a stick.

Work in the Kitchen

In the fall, the farmers pick corn.
They keep the corn for the winter.

Millie's Wonderful Day

Grandpa called Millie.

He said, "Come walk with me.
I have something to show you.
The sky is bright and shiny.
It is a wonderful fall day."

"Is this the day we will eat my sunflower seeds?" asked Millie.

"You will see," Grandpa said.

Millie went up with Grandpa.
She saw that Grandpa was right.
The sky was bright blue.
It was a wonderful day for a walk.

Millie and Grandpa saw the farmer in the field.

Grandpa said, "See, the farmer is picking corn."

Millie asked, "Will he see me?
I am scared, Grandpa."

Grandpa said, "Don't be scared.
Let's go look into the kitchen to see what the farmer does with the corn."

The bird called from the sky, "Hello! Where are you going on this wonderful, bright day?"

Grandpa said, "We are going to see what the farmers do with the corn. Come with us to the kitchen."

Millie and Grandpa walked behind the bird.
All three looked into the kitchen.
They saw corn on the kitchen table.
They saw a glass jar by the corn.

"Tell me what the farmers are doing," said Millie.

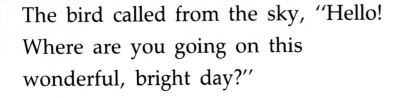

The bird said, "First the farmers cut
the corn.
Next they put it into hot water.
Then they put it into glass jars."

Grandpa said, "Winter is coming soon.
The farmers want corn for the winter.
So they keep it in glass jars on the
kitchen shelf."

Millie saw the boy eat some corn.

She said, "He is eating some
corn right now!
Can we eat now too?"

Grandpa said, "Yes, Millie.
It is time to eat your seeds.
Let's go to your sunflower field!"

Millie ran to her field.

She called to the bird, "You
come too.
I will give you some seeds to eat."

In the sunflower field, Grandpa
picked a wonderful sunflower.
The three sat in the bright
sun eating Millie's seeds.

"What a wonderful day!" said Millie.

Jars for Millie

Grandpa came into the kitchen.

He said, "It is raining out.
The sky is not bright, and my coat
is all wet.
It is a wonderful day to work in
the kitchen."

Millie asked, "Is it a winter day?"

"No, but winter will come soon.
It will snow.
Then we will go to sleep.
So let's get to work," said Grandpa.

"We have some wonderful seeds!"
said Millie.

Grandpa said, "Let's put them
into glass jars.
The jars are on that shelf."

Millie went to get the jars from the
kitchen shelf.

She said, "We will have a shelf of
glass jars like the farmers have."

Grandpa worked and said, "Yes.
We will have jars of seeds on the
kitchen shelf all winter."

Millie put the glass jars of seeds
back on the kitchen shelf.

She said, "This is wonderful.
Now all the seeds are in jars."

Grandpa said, "We worked hard.
Let's sit down."

The two walked out of the kitchen.
They sat down.

"Tell me what you did to grow
sunflowers," said Grandpa.

"I'll show you," said Millie.

This is what Millie made.

Millie Grows Sunflowers

1. I put seeds in the ground.

2. I watered the seeds.

3. Wonderful sunflowers came up in my field!

Grandpa said, "Millie, you did a
wonderful job growing sunflowers.
Now we will have wonderful jars of
seeds next spring."

Millie said, "I need to sleep.
Will you sing to me, Grandpa?"

Grandpa started singing.

"Winter comes with snow, snow, snow.
Millie, off to sleep you go.
Wet snow, wet snow, from the sky,
Comes as winter days go by."

And Millie went to sleep.

Section Two

What I Like

I Like Museums

A museum has wonderful things for people to see and do. It has things from long ago. It has new things too. People go to a museum to have fun.

45

No Lap for Peter

One day, Peter saw Dave Dinosaur on a show. Dave was reading a book. Some children sat on Dave's lap as he read. Dave asked the children sitting on his lap to wave. Peter waved back.

Dave said, "I'll see you next time, boys and girls. Have a good day!"

Peter said, "I like Dave Dinosaur. I wonder where I can find Dave. I want to sit on his lap. I want to read my picture books to Dave."

Just then, Peter's mother and Ann walked in.

Peter asked, "Mom, how can I find a dinosaur?"

"You can see a dinosaur when we go to the museum. A big dinosaur is by the museum wall," said Mom.

Peter said, "Good! That must be Dave. I'll get some books to read to Dave. I wonder what books he likes."

Mom and Ann did not know who Dave Dinosaur was. So they wondered what Peter was planning. They saw Peter go to the shelf of books next to the wall. He picked out some picture books. But Mother and Ann did not know why.

The next day, Peter put his books into the car.

Ann asked, "Why are you putting books into the car, Peter? We are going to the museum now."

Peter said, "I want my books in the car. I'll need them at the museum. I will sit on the dinosaur's soft lap and read."

Ann looked at Peter in a funny way. Everybody stepped into the car. In the car, Peter read all the way to the museum.

At the museum, Peter stepped out of the car. He waved to the dinosaur by the museum wall. But the dinosaur did not wave back. Peter stopped waving. He ran to look.

Peter said, "This dinosaur is big and green. But he has no soft lap! This is not Dave Dinosaur. How can I sit on his soft lap if he has no soft lap?"

"What will you do now?" asked Mom.

Peter sat down on the dinosaur.

He said, "I have my book. And here is a dinosaur. If Dave is not here, I will have to read to this dinosaur."

Peter looked at the dinosaur. Then he started to read.

Sit Here
Talk
to the
Dinosaur

MUSEU

At the Museum

Some people come to this **museum** to learn. Everybody comes to have fun. First, people pick up a map. They save the map. It helps them find things from long ago. A map on the wall helps them find new things too.

Along the wall, people see an animal bone. It is a **dinosaur bone.**

Dinosaurs lived long ago. The bones here show how big one dinosaur was long ago. A farmer saw the bones in his field. Some people put the bones together to make this dinosaur.

In the first picture, people see a
baby **chicken.** Everybody hears a little
tap. Everybody wonders when the next
little chicken will poke its head out.
Then tap, tap, tap, and out comes a new
baby chicken! A boy waves to it.

The chickens in the next picture are
two days old. They are soft and yellow.
They look for something to eat.

The chickens are new. Where is
something old from long ago? Don't you
wonder how people lived long ago?

This house shows how a family lived long ago. People can walk into this house. They see it has just one room with four walls. Long ago, a family lived in a house like this. They made the table and chairs. They made soft beds. They made a small, soft bed for the baby. Long ago, people made all the things in the house.

   People made the new things in this
room. The games are fun to play.
Everybody takes a turn. Everybody
wonders how the games work.

   A museum has so much to see and do.
It has old dinosaur bones. It has new,
soft baby chickens. It has things from
long ago. It has things that are new.
A museum has something for everybody!

I Like Farm Animals

    Some farmers own animals and keep them on a farm. Some animals live in a barn. The farmers feed and take care of the animals they own.

Sarah's Wish

Sarah lived on a farm. Day after day, she wished for a horse. She wanted a small horse of her own.

One day, Sarah went into the barn. She saw Dad feeding a cow. She saw the horses. She wished she owned one.

She waved to the horses and said,
"I have a wish I wish to say,
I wish to own a horse some day."

Dad said, "Did I hear you say you want a horse of your own? You don't know how to take care of a horse."

Sarah said, "I can learn. A horse is a good pet. I can take good care of it."

Dad said, "We will see. Follow me. You can help me feed the chickens. Then I'll show you how to take care of the horses."

Sarah said, "Good. I know how to take care of the small chickens."

Sarah picked up some corn. Then she followed Dad out of the barn. Sarah put some corn on the ground. All the small chickens followed her. They came to nibble. They nibbled and nibbled. They ate all the corn.

Dad said, "You are doing a fine job, Sarah. You work here. I must feed the cows. Then I'll go out to the field. I have to see how a horse is doing."

Sarah said, "I want to go with you.
But I'll work here. I'll take care of
the small chickens. I'll see the
horse in the field soon."

Nibble, nibble, nibble went the
chickens. Sarah gave them more corn.

As they ate, Sarah said,
"I have a wish I wish to say,
I wish to own a horse some day."

Day after day, Sarah followed Dad as he worked in the barn. She learned to feed the cows. She learned to give oats to the horses. And day after day, Dad went to see the horse in the field.

One day, Dad said, "Sarah, some time ago you said you wanted a horse. Now you know how to take care of one. So follow me out to the field. I have a secret to show you."

Sarah wondered what the secret was. She followed Dad to the field. A small foal was in the field!

Dad said, "Now you have a small horse of your own. You can take care of it."

Sarah patted the small foal and said, "Now I am so happy to say, I have a horse of my own this day!"

A Name for the Foal

Sarah liked her new horse. She liked how it followed her around in the field.

Late one morning, Sarah asked Dad to pack a lunch for her. She wanted to have lunch with her foal. Dad packed a good lunch. He packed an apple for Sarah. He packed one for the foal too.

Out in the field, Sarah ate the lunch Dad packed for her. She gave her foal some oats. She gave it the apple Dad packed. The foal ate it.

Sarah said, "Foal, you need a name. What is a good name for you?"

The foal did not say what it wanted for a name.

The next day was a fine day. Sarah went to the barn. She gave oats to the horses and corn to the cows.

Sarah wondered what to name her foal. So she asked the cows.

She said, "My foal is small. It is soft and brown. It eats oats. What can I name it?"

The cows did not say what to name her foal. They just ate the corn.

Dad walked into the barn.

Sarah said, "Dad, my foal has no name. What is a good name for it?"

Dad said, "You have a fine, small foal. It needs a fine name. It was my secret pet for you."

"Secret! That is a fine name. I'll name my foal Secret! I'll tack up its name on the gate for people to see," said Sarah.

Sarah tacked up Secret's new name. She gave Secret some oats. Secret ate all of the oats.

Sarah said, "Secret, now you have a name of your own. How do you like it?"

Secret jumped and kicked when Sarah
said its name. Sarah laughed.

"Secret likes its new name just
fine," said Sarah.

"Secret likes you, too," said Dad.

Foal

by Mary Britton Miller

Come trotting up
Beside your mother,
Little skinny.

Lay your neck across
Her back, and whinny,
Little foal.

You think you're a horse
Because you can trot—
But you're not.

Your eyes are so wild,
And each leg is as tall
As a pole;

And you're only a skittish
Child, after all,
Little foal.

Just for You

Make a picture of an animal that makes
a funny pet. Give your pet a name of
its own. Is your pet small? Is it big?
Is it hard? Is it soft? Did it live long
ago? Does it live now? Put My Pet on
the top of your picture. Tell why you
want this funny pet for your own.

I Like Camp

At camp, children can play soccer. They can learn to play on a team. They can learn to swim too. Pablo and Lynn tell what they do at camp.

My Days at Camp

Hello everybody!

I am fine. I don't have much to say today. But Mr. Carson from camp says we have to tell you how we are. What he says, we do!

It was fun playing soccer today. My soccer team made one goal in today's game. I wanted to win. But we did not win. We need to work on getting that soccer ball into the goal!

I like this camp. But I don't like what we have to eat! I always wonder what you are having to eat.

Pablo

Hello Mom,

I always eat all my corn at lunch. I know that makes you happy. I don't like it. So I always eat it last!

It was warm today. Nine of us followed Mr. Carson on a hike. We hiked around camp. We saw some small ducks by the lake. They followed us!

After today's hike, the nine of us kicked soccer balls around. We kicked more balls into the goal than last time.

Soon we will play a team from a camp far away. I want my team to win! I know we can win!

Pablo

Hello Dad,

   It was still warm today. We played a
soccer game. All the people at camp
came to see us play. They always like
to see us play. They want us to win.

   They called, "Win, team, win. Go,
team, go. Kick the ball into the goal."

   But we still did not win.

   One boy put a frog in my warm bed.
Now I'll always look as I jump into bed!

   I wonder where that boy sleeps!
                              Pablo

Hello everybody!

Today, at last, my soccer team did win! We needed four goals to win. I made the last goal. That helped us win!

After winning the game, we all followed Mr. Carson. We went to the kitchen for pizza. Nine of us sat at one table. The pizza was good!

Mr. Carson says that the nine of us are always together. He calls us "The Fine Nine." That is fine with me!

Thanks for letting me come to camp.

Pablo

The Big Show

Hello from camp!

I am having a good time here. Today I met a new girl. We like to go to the pool together.

On warm days, we always swim at the pool. On cold days, we always go hiking. I am learning how to swim. So I like the warm days. I always like to swim more than hike!

We always like to be up late. We plan the big show we will have. Everybody will do something they learned at camp. I wonder what I'll do.

Please pet my dog for me.

Lynn

Hello family,

How is my dog? I always wonder if you are feeding her.

Today a small snake came into the room as we ate. It was so small, but everybody was scared. I laughed. I was standing by the door, so I let the snake out. We all followed it out. We saw it go into the field.

Today everybody worked on the big show. Nine children made puppets. Some people worked on a game to show us.

I still wonder what I can do in the show.

Lynn

Hello Mom and Dad,

   It was still warm out today. It was
a fine day for swimming. Mr. Brown
showed us how to float. After we
learned to float, we all started to
splash water. We kicked in the warm
water. It was fun splashing in the
pool on a warm day.

   We splashed water on the boys. Then
they splashed on us. Mr. Brown did not
like the splashing. But still, he did
say we did a fine job floating.

   Now I know what I'll do in the show.

   Today I lost my soft, little bear.
At last, I saw it in a stack of lost
things at the pool. It was still fine.

                     Lynn

Hello everybody!

Today was the big show. It was a fine, warm day for a show. First we marched around the camp. We followed Mr. Brown as we marched. It was like a little hike with music! Marching made us so warm. I wanted to jump into the pool!

Next, everybody came to the pool. Nine of us jumped into the pool with a splash. Then we floated in the water. We floated this way and that way. We floated around in a ring. Music played. We splashed to the music. All nine of us put on a good water show.

Lynn

Hello family,

Today is my last day at camp. We made pictures of camp. We went for one last hike together. We went swimming in the warm water.

How can it be time to go? We just came not long ago. I like going to camp. Now I'll always want to come back.

Say hello to my dog. I'll be back soon. I'll be happy to be back in my own soft, warm bed!

Lynn

Think of That!

Imagine a Way

What would you do if you did not like something the way it was? You would imagine ways to make it better. We imagine, because it helps us find a better way to do something.

ZOO

79

Rings for a Raccoon

Long ago, raccoons did not yet have stripes on them. Randy Raccoon lived in the zoo. But he was not happy. People did not come to look at Randy. So he went looking for them. He saw many people looking at Zeke the zebra. So Randy went to talk to Zeke.

Randy said, "Zeke, I want to have stripes like the ones you have. Many people like zebras better than raccoons. They like to look at you, because you have stripes. I don't have any stripes. Imagine how good I would look with stripes! Would you help me?"

Zeke said, "Randy, I am very proud of my stripes. I have stripes, because I am a zebra. You don't need stripes, because you are a raccoon. Stripes look better on zebras than they would on raccoons. You can be very proud of how you look. It is better for you to look like a raccoon than a zebra."

Randy said, "But I want stripes so people will come to look at me. I don't need as many as you have. I just want to be proud of how I look. I know I'll look better with stripes."

"Then I'll paint some stripes on you," said Zeke.

"Painting stripes on me will not help very much. That will not help, because when I go swimming, the stripes will float away," said Randy.

"Then let's imagine what would work better. I know! We can make stripes. I'll paste them on you. You will be a raccoon with stripes yet," said the zebra.

Randy said, "Pasting stripes on me will not work, because the stripes will blow away when I run."

Zeke and Randy Raccoon sat down. They sat very still. Zeke looked at his own stripes.

Zeke said, "I don't want to give all my stripes away. I am too proud of them. Yet I do have more than I need. So I'll give you some of them. Put them on. See how you look with them. You will have stripes yet."

The zebra gave the raccoon some of his stripes. Randy made little rings from them. He put them on. He looked better than he imagined he would! Randy was very proud of his new stripes.

Now all raccoons have stripes. The stripes are called rings. All raccoons have rings, because one zebra helped!

Too Many Vegetables

Mrs. Kent lived in a house in the city. She did not have children of her own, but many children liked her. Mrs. Kent was like a grandma to everybody.

Mrs. Kent was cleaning. Joey came to the door. She let Joey in.

Joey said, "Hello! I have some vegetables for you. My dad and I picked them this morning. We are so proud that we can grow them. We wanted to give some to you."

Mrs. Kent said, "You must be very proud of your work. Thank you. I'll cook the vegetables today."

Joey went out the door. Soon Kathy, who lived next door, stopped by.

She said, "Hello, Mrs. Kent. I have some corn for you. Mom and I went shopping today. We wanted to give you some corn, because it looked so good. You don't have any yet, do you?"

Mrs. Kent said, "No, I don't have any corn yet. Thank you very much. I'll cook it today."

After Kathy went out the door, Mrs. Kent said, "I can not imagine how I'll eat so many vegetables. I'll have to cook them today."

Soon, a van stopped by Mrs. Kent's house. Out of the van came Tom and Tina with a box of vegetables! They came in with the box.

Tom said, "Mrs. Kent, we went out to a farm this morning. We have a box of vegetables for us and a box for you. We know how you like vegetables."

Mrs. Kent said, "I like cooking and eating them. Thank you for the box of vegetables."

Tom and Tina went back to the van. Mrs. Kent went to the kitchen. She looked at the box of vegetables.

She wondered, "What will I cook? How can I eat so many vegetables?"

Zap! Just like that, Mrs. Kent imagined what she would do.

She said, "Soup, soup, soup! I'll cook vegetable soup! I'll ask the children to come back. We will all eat vegetable soup together."

So Mrs. Kent cooked. The children came back. And they all ate vegetable soup together!

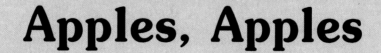

Apples, Apples

Apples grow on apple trees. Once apple seeds are planted in the ground, trees grow. Year after year, the apple trees grow and blossom. Imagine all we can do with apples!

Apples to Eat

A man named Johnny Appleseed lived many years ago. He was a kind and gentle man. He was kind to people. He was gentle with animals.

Once Johnny was eating an apple. He looked at the circle of seeds in it. Johnny imagined what it would be like to have fields of apple trees. He planned to walk through fields to plant apple seeds. So he saved the apple seeds to plant. And that is just what he did.

First Johnny went to an apple mill to get seeds. He picked out some apple seeds. Once he picked them out, he saved them to plant.

Johnny walked through fields planting the seeds. He stopped to give seeds to people. He would tell them how to care for the pretty trees that would grow.

Some people said they would know who walked through a field, because they saw a man with a pan on his head. It was Johnny! He cooked with the pan when it was time to eat. Imagine how funny he looked walking through fields!

People liked Johnny, because he was kind to them. They liked his gentle ways. He helped them make new houses. People helped by giving Johnny something to eat and drink.

Johnny liked being kind to animals. As he walked through the fields, he stopped to talk to them. He was gentle with them. He helped them find water to drink. He did not scare them. The animals liked his gentle ways.

After many years, Johnny went back to see the apple trees he planted. In the spring, he saw the trees bud. Many buds came out on the trees. After budding, the trees blossomed. Fluffy, white blossoms came from the buds. The fluffy, blossoming trees looked pretty. They looked fluffy and white.

Buds   Blossoms   Apples

Soon the fluffy, white blossoms came falling to the ground. Once the fluffy, white blossoms came down, apples started to grow. The apples started to grow where buds once blossomed.

In the fall, Johnny saw pretty, red apples on the trees. He was proud of his work.

When Johnny was old, he stopped
walking through fields to plant seeds.
Now many people did what Johnny once
did. They planted trees. They saw
them grow. They saw the trees bud with
fluffy blossoms. After many years,
people ate apples from the pretty trees.

Now we have many apples to eat.
Imagine that!

What Can You Do with an Apple?

We can make many kinds of things from apples. Years ago, children made apple puppets because they wanted something to play with. Some people still make them today.

We can look into an apple. See what
it looks like. It is white. It has a
circle of seeds in it. We can take the
seeds out of the circle. We can
plant them. Do you know what will grow?

We can make pretty pictures with
apple seeds. We take the seeds from a
cup. Then we paste them in little
circles. The circles of seeds make
a shape.

The children here make pictures with apples and paint. They make many kinds of shapes from the apple. They put the apple shapes into cups of red and cups of white paint. They make pretty pictures. The children are proud of the pictures they make.

We eat and drink things made from apples, because they are good. We can cook them. We can drink a cup of apple drink. When we drink a cup of apple drink, we know it once came from an apple. Would you like a cup of apple drink?

We can eat an apple! What a
wonderful thing to do with one! We have
many kinds of apples, because Johnny
Appleseed once walked through fields to
plant seeds. What kind of apples do
you like?

What kinds of things can you
imagine to do with an apple?

Apple Blossoms

by Ralph Bergengren

There is a day
   That comes in spring
When apple trees
   Are blossoming.
They blossom out
   So quick some morn
It's like a giant
   Popping corn.

Just for You

Imagine you live in an apple house.
Cut out a big, red apple shape. Is it
round like a circle? Make your apple
look like a house. Make a door to walk
through. What kinds of things can you
put on your house? Tell what it would
be like to live in an apple. You can
be proud of your work.

The Wonderful Apple

by Nancy Ross Ryan

Long ago, Kara lived with her family on a farm. Day after day, Kara worked in the fields. But she was not very happy. The sun was hot. The work was hard. And Kara's two proud sisters would not help her with her work.

One day, a woman with a bright cap walked through the field to talk to her.

The woman said, "Hello, little one. I have walked all day. I need something to eat. Will you help me?"

Kara said, "Come with me. I will get some warm cakes for you."

The two went to the house together.

After the woman ate, she said, "Many thanks to you. You are very kind. Your mother and father must be very proud of you. Now what can I do to help you?"

Kara said, "I would like something to make me happy as I work in the field."

The woman patted Kara on the back. Then she walked away.

The very next day, Father came in with a sack of many things. He gave his two big girls coats they needed. He gave Kara a pretty, red apple in a cup.

He said, "A woman gave this to me in the city. She said to give it to you."

The two sisters laughed at Kara's new apple. But Kara was proud of it.

Once Kara turned the apple in the cup, the apple started singing. What pretty music it made! Time after time, the apple would sing of secret caves, fields far away, and still, blue lakes. What wonderful things Kara imagined as the apple was singing! Day after day, Kara would sing along with the apple as she worked in the field.

When Kara's sisters saw how happy the apple's music made her, they wanted to hear it too. So Kara gave the apple to one of them. The sister played with it. She ran with the apple. Then pop! Ping! She dropped it on a stake in the ground. At once, the music stopped. The apple did not play any more music.

For many days, Kara worked hard in the field. But she was not happy. She wanted to hear the apple sing once more.

Kara sat down by a tree, out of the hot sun. Once more, she saw the woman walking through the field.

The woman asked, "Where is your wonderful apple?"

Kara said, "The apple does not work. It does not sing, because it was dropped in the field."

Then the woman said, "Little one. You don't need the apple. You have all you need to make you happy. You know how to sing just like the apple did. And you can still imagine pretty pictures that the music helped you imagine. Be happy and sing with me."

With that, the woman started singing. Soon Kara was singing along with her. And she was happy once more.

Books to Read

Frog and Toad Together by Arnold Lobel

Frog and Toad plant seeds. Read to find out what kind of seeds they plant.

Dinosaur Time by Peggy Parish

Dinosaurs once lived long ago. How many of the dinosaur names do you know?

Apple Pigs by Ruth Orbach

What do you do when you have too many apples? Read this book to find out.

Section Four

Having Fun

Making Things

It is fun to make things. Then we don't have to buy them. We can cut, paste, and paint. We might even make something by cooking it on the stove.

Birthday Pancakes

Jeff and Sue planned to make something to eat for Mom's birthday.

Sue asked, "What can we cook?"

"Let's make pancakes," said Jeff.

Sue said, "That might be fun! We can make birthday pancakes. Let's keep it a secret from Mom. I'll buy the things we need. I'll buy milk and pancake mix."

Sue went to buy milk and pancake mix.

The next morning, Jeff and Sue started making pancakes. But soon Mom started for the kitchen. Jeff stopped her by the door. He would not even let her take another step.

Mom asked, "Well, what is this?"

Jeff said, "Happy Birthday, Mom! Sue and I are cooking for you today. Please don't come into the kitchen. We don't want you to see what we are making."

Mom said, "Well, then I'll go out to buy milk. We might need more milk today. I'll be back soon."

Mom wondered if Jeff and Sue might make a birthday cake. Would they spill mix on the stove and make a mess?

In the kitchen, Sue read, "Begin by mixing one cup of pancake mix with one cup of milk. Put in the things you see in the picture. Mix it well. Put a pan on the stove. When the pan begins to get hot, put circles of mix in the pan. Cook the pancakes. When they begin to get brown, turn them. Then cook them even more."

As the two mixed, milk spilled. As they cooked, pancake mix spilled. It made a mess on the stove. Pancake mix even splashed on the wall! What a mess!

The cooks worked fast to clean up the mess. Mom came back. Then the two came out of the kitchen with pancakes.

Mom said, "You made birthday pancakes! You did well! But how big a mess is in the kitchen? Did you spill on the stove?"

Sue laughed and said, "We just spilled a little on the stove. But we cleaned up the mess."

Mom ate a pancake and said, "This is even better than birthday cake! And I can even make a wish!"

The Make-It School

Children come to this school to make
things. They come to make pictures.
The children make what they
want. They come, because they
know they will begin another day of fun.
They even get to keep what they make.

The children begin to work on many kinds of things. One girl makes a puppet. She makes it from a sack. Another girl has a new pet fish. So she paints a picture of it. She does well! You can tell she is proud of her painting. She might have to clean up a mess if she spills any paint.

Children here make pins. They make them from thin circles of tin. They don't even have to buy pins. They know how to make them. The pins are not like one another. The children put the pins on. They put the pins together well.

Some children don't know what to make. They begin by taking some of this and some of that. They make a pretty picture.

What do the children do with the things they make? One might pin them up on a wall. Another might even give them away. Some children like the things they make so well, they might even want to keep them.

The children will come back another day. They know they will make something new next time.

Making Music

We can learn how to play an instrument so we can make music. A drum, a trumpet, and cymbals are some of the many instruments we might play.

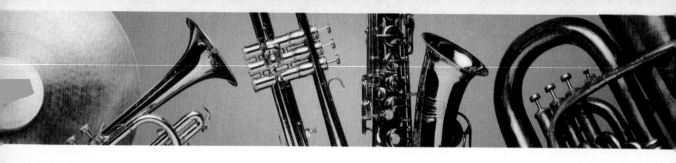

The Parade

The city parade would begin soon. People walked and came on bikes to see it. They lined up to see it well. They knew the parade would be good.

Everybody that had instruments was beginning to line up too. Children on bikes went to see the instruments. Carlo followed the children on bikes. He stepped from his bike to look. Today he would pick the instrument he wanted to learn to play.

He said, "Some day I want to play an instrument in a parade. First I want to see them all. Then I will pick one."

Carlo and his mother sat down. Carlo knew the parade would begin soon. He knew he would soon hear the beat of the drum. He knew he would see line after line of instruments going by.

Just then, a man called out, "Strike up the music! Beat the drums! Strike the cymbals! Begin the parade!"

The parade started. Carlo looked at all the instruments. He saw people beat the drums. He saw a girl strike the cymbals as she went by.

Carlo said, "The cymbals might be fun to play, since everybody would hear me strike them together."

Then the parade stopped. People stopped beating the drums. People stopped striking the cymbals. The lines of people stopped right by Carlo.

At first, only one boy put his trumpet up to his lips. He played some music. Then more people that had trumpets played. The music made people want to sing.

Carlo said, "A trumpet might even be fun to play. I would play a trumpet with my lips. I would need good lips to play it."

Next, Carlo saw something funny in the parade. He saw a man riding by on a float. The man was playing a piano.

Carlo wondered, "Why is a piano in a parade? Playing a piano in a parade might be fun, since I would not have to march. I would be the only one riding in the parade as I played my instrument. I would spend my day playing the only piano in the parade."

Carlo did not know what instrument he wanted to play. But he knew he wanted to make music.

An Instrument for Carlo

Carlo went to his house on his bike. He put his bike away and went in.

Mom asked Carlo, "Which instrument do you want to learn how to play?"

Carlo said, "Well, I don't know. I like the way the trumpets shine. I would put the trumpet up to my lips and play. I like the cymbals, since everybody can hear them. Beating the drums would be fun. I like the piano. But we would spend too much to buy one."

128

"Since you will play the instrument, pick the one you want. I'll take care of the spending," said Mom.

Carlo said, "I pick the trumpet. It will be fun to play a shiny instrument. I'll make people want to sing."

Mom laughed. She went into another room. Carlo followed her. Then Mom gave Carlo a trumpet.

She said, "I played this when I was little. I marched in parades. I had to dip my trumpet up and down as I marched. I have not even played it since then."

Carlo said, "You played the trumpet?"

Mom said, "Yes. And since you want to play the trumpet, we don't have to spend a thing."

Carlo said, "I would have picked the trumpet right away, but I did not know you had one."

Mom said, "Well, I wanted you to pick the instrument you wanted. Now you can learn to play the trumpet well. You can march in a parade like the one we saw today."

"That will be fun! Now I have a trumpet that is mine!" said Carlo.

Carlo picked up his trumpet to shine it up. Soon he would begin to learn to play music on his own trumpet.

Carlo put the trumpet up to his lips. He gave a big blow. But only a little "pop" came out. He knew he had some things to learn.

Lewis Has a Trumpet

by Karla Kuskin

A trumpet
A trumpet
Lewis has a trumpet
A bright one that's yellow
A loud proud horn
He blows it in the evening
When the moon is newly rising
He blows it when it's raining
In the cold and misty morn
It honks and it whistles
It roars like a lion
It rumbles like a lion
With a wheezy huffing hum
His parents say it's awful
Oh really simply awful
But Lewis says he loves it
It's such a handsome trumpet
And when he's through with trumpets
He's going to buy a drum.

Just for You

Make an instrument. You don't need
to spend a thing. You don't need to put
it up to your lips. You don't need to
beat it like a drum. You only need
water, a stick, and glass jars. Begin
by getting four glass jars. Put one jar
after another in a line.

1. Put only a little water
   in a jar.

2. Put more water in the
   next jar.

3. Put some more water in the next jar.

4. Put even more water in the last jar.

Tap, don't strike, the jars with a small stick. Spend some time tapping one glass after another. See if you can make music.

Making People Laugh

A clown puts on a funny wig, a
costume, and makeup. Clowns make
people laugh.

At the Fair

Brian and Mark wanted to go to the fair to put on clown makeup. They went with Mother to the car. They saw Mr. Taylor, who had once lived next door. He spoke to the boys.

Mr. Taylor said, "Hello, boys! I am going to work at the fair. If you have enough time, come and see me. Maybe you can help me with my work."

The boys waved. They knew it would be fun to help Mr. Taylor.

At the fair, Brian and Mark looked for Mr. Taylor. They did not see where he was working. But they did see a clown putting makeup on people. The people looked like clowns. Brian and Mark wanted to look like clowns too.

Mark asked the clown, "Will you put clown makeup on us?"

The clown said, "Yes. That is not a hard task for Sam the clown. I have some good clown makeup for you. Sit down by the mirror. I'll start now. You can see how you look in the mirror."

Mark saw a clock next to Sam's mirror. The funny clock had white paper wings on it. Mark spoke as he sat down.

He asked, "Why does that clock have wings on it?"

Sam said, "Well, time will fly by. That clock tells me that maybe I'll have enough time to put makeup on you. I must not be late for the clown show."

Mark laughed at the funny clock. Sam put white makeup on Mark. He also put a funny, red wig on Mark. Mark started to look like a clown.

Then Sam put makeup on Brian, also.

Sam said, "Nose, nose, put on a nose.
Maybe a red nose would go well. Wig,
wig, pick out a wig."

Sam put a big, red nose on Brian.
Sam also put a blue wig on Brian. Brian
looked in the mirror. He laughed.

Sam said, "Good. Now you both
look enough like clowns to do a task for
me in the show. Come back at one."

The boys walked away. They knew they
still had to find Mr. Taylor.

The Clown Show

The boys came back to help Sam in the show. They had to stop looking for Mr. Taylor. They looked at the clock. It was time for the clown show. They wanted to know what task Sam had for them to do. Sam spoke to the boys.

Sam said, "It takes skill to be a clown. Some people spend years to learn the skill of being one."

He said, "This task is not hard. You have enough skill now to do well enough for this show. You have makeup on, so you don't need a mask. You have red noses. But you do need costumes. Here are costumes to put on. Maybe they will make you look even more like clowns."

Mark and Brian put on the costumes. They looked in the mirror. They looked very good in the costumes. Sam spoke.

He said, "Now I have tasks for you. I'll give you two pails. In the show, I'll tell you to throw water on me. But you will not throw water. You will only throw this white paper. No one will get wet. Then maybe everybody will laugh."

Brian said, "We can do that. That is not a hard task. Throwing paper does not take much skill."

Sam said, "Good. Maybe you can also help me with another task. You can help me when I spin the cups. That will be enough help for this show.

"Take another look in the mirror. Does your nose look funny enough? Your costumes are fine. Let's go," Sam said.

Brian wanted to play a joke on Sam. When Sam was not looking, Brian put water in his pail. Then the boys went to the show. Sam spoke to the children.

He said, "Hello, boys and girls. I'll start by showing you my skill of spinning cups on sticks. Call out if you see one that might stop spinning."

Mark and Brian gave the cups to Sam.

Sam started spinning the cups. Children spoke out when they saw one falling. Sam showed his skill. He ran to spin the cup just in time. Then another cup stopped spinning. Sam ran to that cup also. But he knew he was too late. The cup came falling down. The children laughed. The boys put the cups away.

Sam called, "You can not catch me!"

The boys knew it was time to throw paper on Sam. Mark chased Sam. He started throwing paper from his pail.

White paper came flying out of Mark's pail. Sam's wig was all white. Sam knew that Brian had paper also. But when Brian came with his pail, water splashed out! Sam was all wet! His makeup started dripping. The boys saw a man they knew. The man with dripping makeup on his skin was Mr. Taylor.

Brian said, "We did find Mr. Taylor! He is working right here! He is Sam!"

Mr. Taylor said, "Yes, I am Sam. What good clowns you are! You even played a funny joke on me!"

Wonderful Water

What is Under Water

Fish live under water. People like to learn about fish and plants that live in the ocean. People swim deep under water to see them.

Why Fish Don't Make Noise

Long ago, no one made any noise. People did not talk. Birds and animals did not make noise. Only the King of Music made noise. He made music.

The King of Music lived in a tree in the woods. Day after day, he played his music for the animals in the woods.

One day, two children knocked on the king's door. When they knocked, the music stopped. The king came out.

The king had on a wonderful jacket. It had many instruments in it. While the king walked to the lake, he talked about the instruments. Wild animals and birds came out of the woods to see them.

The king said, "You need to make noises of your own. I'll play some instruments from my jacket. While I play, pick a noise of your own."

The king got the first instrument from his jacket. He played the small, shiny instrument. The birds liked the music. But the fish under water did not even hear it. The birds picked singing as a way to make noise.

The king got a second instrument from his jacket. What a big noise it made! The big, wild animals liked the second instrument, so they made big noises.

The little, wild animals of the woods wanted noises too. The king got a third instrument from his jacket. The third instrument made soft noises. The little, wild animals of the woods liked the soft noises of the third instrument. So they walked into the woods making soft noises.

The children did not know which noise to pick.

The king said, "You can take all the noises of the instruments in my jacket."

The children liked the plan. They started talking. Then they started singing. They made big noises like the second, big instrument. And they made soft noises like the third instrument. The children walked into the woods, happy that they got to sing, talk, and make noise.

The king got down to see the fish under water. He wondered what noise they would pick. Under water, the fish did not hear any noises. They saw the king move his lips while he talked. They saw the children and wild animals. They saw the king play his first, second, and third instruments. But they did not hear any noise. So to this day, fish don't make noise. People sing and talk. Wild animals make noises. But fish only look as if they are talking.

Jacques Cousteau

Jacques Cousteau likes learning about the ocean. He likes to see what is deep under water. He spends time on a boat finding out about the ocean. Then he writes books about what he learns.

As a boy, Jacques liked to swim. He would jump from the dock. Then he would swim deep under water. While he was under water, he got to see many kinds of fish, plants, and rocks.

As time went on, Jacques wanted to learn about the fish, plants, and rocks in the ocean. He wanted to write books about them. So he went swimming deep under water to learn.

Jacques liked the fish he saw under water. Some fish had spots. Some had stripes. Jacques would catch some fish in a kind of pot. Then he would write about them.

Jacques looked at some bright plants
growing under water. Fish went
swimming around the bright plants.

While Jacques was under water, he
also looked at some animals that live in
the ocean. He would take pictures of
the animals he saw. He put the pictures
in the books he was writing. He wanted
people to see what was in the ocean.

Jacques Cousteau made a house deep under water. At the house, people learn about the ocean. They swim deep under water around the house. They learn about animals and plants that live in the ocean.

Jacques has learned many things about the ocean. He still writes about the wonderful things under water!

Just for You

Here are some knock, knock jokes. You will need two people. One of you reads the first line. The second one reads the second line.

1. Knock, knock.
Who is it?
   Water.
Water who?
   Water you doing today?

2. Knock, knock.
Who is it?
   Also.
Also who?
   Also the hole in your jacket for you.

We Need Water

People and animals need water. We need water to drink. Some animals need water to drink and some live in it. We wash windows with water. We need water to scrub things clean.

The Dog Wash

Beth was going to help Katy wash the windows on the garage. Beth got the tub from the garage while Katy got the hose. Fluffy saw the girls getting the tub and the hose from the garage. She followed Katy and the hose.

As Katy walked out of the garage, she said, "Look at Fluffy! It looks as though we need to put her into the tub right now. But even though she needs a good scrubbing, we don't have time to wash her today."

Beth said, "We will have to scrub her another day. We already have enough to do to last a whole day."

The girls started washing the garage windows. First Katy scrubbed one whole window. Then Beth sprayed it with the hose. As the girls scrubbed the garage windows, Fluffy jumped in the spray.

Beth and Katy had already scrubbed two whole windows, when Fluffy saw a girl with a balloon. The girl waved to Fluffy. As she did, her balloon floated away. Fluffy chased after the balloon. Beth and Katy laughed as Fluffy jumped at the balloon.

The balloon floated by the tub of water. Fluffy looked only at the bright balloon. She did not see the tub. She jumped up. Splash! She went right into the water! Fluffy shook water all around. Katy and Beth got wet from the spray.

Katy said, "It looks as though we can wash Fluffy now. She is already in the tub!"

Beth scrubbed Fluffy while Katy sprayed water from the hose. Then Katy put the hose down. Fluffy shook water all around.

Beth said, "Well, we already did a whole day's work! We washed some windows, and because of that balloon, Fluffy got clean too!"

Go Away!

One hot day, Goat went to the lake to drink. The water was cold as it went down Goat's throat. While Goat was drinking, Frog jumped out of the water.

Frog called, "Go away, Goat! You are drinking my whole lake! I was already here. Don't drink while I am here."

Goat said, "Please let me drink. I just need some water to wet my throat on this hot day."

Frog said, "Even though you need water for your throat, I don't want you here. I want to take a nap in the sun. I don't want a goat here while I sleep. Now you have got to go!"

Goat shook his head and walked away.

Just then, a boy thin as a pole walked by. He had a big box. It looked to Frog as though the boy wanted to catch a frog. Frog shook when he saw the box.

The boy stepped into the water to catch Frog. But Frog splashed away. Water sprayed all around.

Goat wondered about the splashing. Though he did not want to, Goat ran back to the lake. By then, the boy had already picked up Frog by the throat!

All at once, Goat ran. He splashed
into the lake. Water sprayed on the
boy. The boy shook from the cold water.
He dropped Frog and ran away. Frog was
so scared, he shook.

Frog said, "Thank you for saving me.
If you had not come along, I would
already be in that box. Take a drink to
wet your throat any time you like. Just
don't drink the whole lake!"

While Goat had some water to wet his
throat, Frog went to sleep in the sun.

Boats Are in Water

Some people work on boats. They might work on a tug and push big boats to the ocean. Some people ride on boats. Before people had a way to fly, they went by boat.

To the North Pole

Matt Henson wanted to win a long, cold race through the ocean. He wanted to be on the team of people to get to the **North Pole** first. Though some people had already started out, no one had made it to the North Pole before.

Matt left for the North Pole with a man named **Robert Peary.** They left together by boat. In 1908, they started the race north.

Matt Henson

Robert Peary

Matt was a good man to go to the North Pole. Before the team even left, Matt already knew many things about places with snow and ice. He knew how to talk to the people who lived in the North. He also helped the team find the way as they led the way to the North Pole. He wanted the team to be first.

The race to the North Pole was hard.
In the cold, the ocean water did not
flow. It turned into ice. When the
water did not flow, the boat did not
move. Even though ice was in the way,
the race had to go on. The team was
already near the North Pole. They did
not give up. They got out of the
boat and went through the snow. Before
the team left the boat in the ice, they
wondered if they would be first.

So the team left the boat behind.
They led the way through ice and snow.
It was 1909 before the team got to the
North Pole. It was a cold place with
snow and ice. No one knows if they made
it first, but Matt Henson and Robert
Peary said they did.

I Work on a Tug

My name is Miss Lee. I work on Tug
Six. It is a good place to work. I
like being where water flows. Though I
must get up before the sun does, I like
my job. I must be on the tug before six
in the morning. At about six, the tug
will push away from the dock.

One man cooks for us on the boat. He goes to work before many people even get up. Today, he is already making pancakes. He flips them. He puts a stack of them on a plate for us to eat.

Before long, we get a call for Tug Six. I help run Tug Six. Though Tug Six is small, we have to move a big boat. It has left the ocean's deep water. Tug Six must get near the big boat to push it to the dock.

Tug Six goes right near the big boat. Before we move it, though, we throw a rope to a man on the big boat. The rope goes up the side of the boat. Then the tug and the big boat are near one another. While water flows around us, the ropes are led into place. Then we push the big boat.

Tug Six does a good job. I help make Tug Six push, turn, and move the big boat. The boat goes by its place near the dock. Tug Six moves through the flowing water. Even though the work is hard, we have fun. Before long, we have already led the boat to its place.

Though we worked hard pushing that boat near the dock, Tug Six has more work left to do. Some flat boats will be led into the docks today. Some also need to be led from the dock to the ocean.

Before the sun goes down, we have already led and pushed many boats through flowing, ocean water. Tug Six goes back to the dock. We will be back to work on the tug the next day.

Jewels Floating By
by Claudia Lewis

The little tugboats
circled with lights—
kings' crowns
cast upon the water.

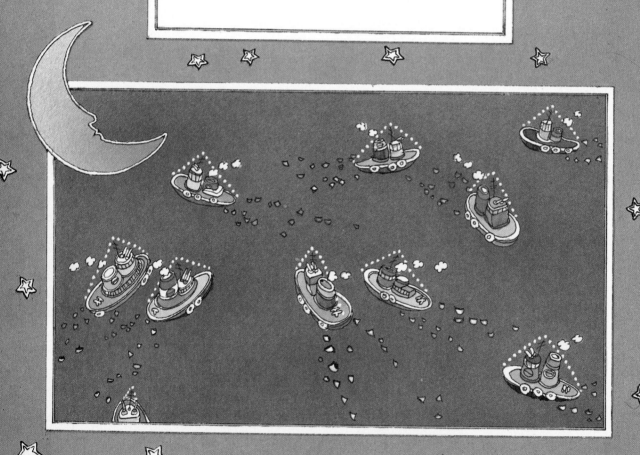

Something to See

See a Pet Show

Some children take their pets to the pet show. Everybody can look at the pets during the show. The children want their pets to win ribbons.

Pets at School

The sign in this room says, "Pet Show Today." Many children have brought their pets for the pet show. Mrs. Fields has asked everybody to tell about their pets.

Stan said, "I brought my fish. It swims around during the day. It makes swimming look so easy."

Jack said, "I brought my tame pet mice. Even though my mice are tame, they can run very fast. You will see the mice running during the show."

Bret said, "I have a turtle. When I put my turtle on the table, it only moves an inch. Even though it will try hard, my turtle does not have an easy time moving fast. It only moves inch by inch by inch."

Jill said, "My tame, little pet has
an old sock. I gave it the sock. It
nibbles on the sock during the day.
Then it makes the sock into a soft bed.
My pet sleeps on the sock. During the
time I sleep, it plays. When I get up
at seven, it goes to sleep on the sock."

Tish said, "I brought my tame bird.
At my house, I try to get it to stand on
my hand. It is easy for my bird to walk
inch by inch along my hand."

Pat said, "My brother brought the puppy today. My brother and I take care of her. My puppy shakes hands with me. When she shakes hands, I pet her."

It is fun to see all the tame pets at school! It is easy to see that the children like telling about their pets. They like learning about new pets too.

Ribbon for a Rabbit

Rosa went with her mom, dad, and brother to the pet show. They brought their pet rabbit, Archie. They wanted Archie to win a ribbon at the show.

Mrs. Gates, a woman at the pet show, talked to them.

She said, "Hello! Make a sign for your pet. Write your pet's name on the sign. Then put the sign next to your pet. Soon I'll hand out ribbons to seven pets who do something well."

Mom and Dad put Archie in a box on the table. Rosa's brother made a sign for Archie. Then Mrs. Gates came to look. She read the sign near Archie.

She asked, "What can Archie do well?"

Rosa said, "That is not easy to say. He does try to be a good rabbit. He does not make noise during the day. He is tame and eats out of my hand. But I don't know how he will win a ribbon."

Mrs. Gates started writing on her paper. She went to see another pet.

Rosa's family left Archie and went to look at the pets. They had to try to find something Archie might learn to do well. Rosa saw seven white mice.

Rosa said, "Mice run fast. They find it easy to run. Maybe Archie can try to run as fast as the mice."

Then Rosa's brother saw a dog making noise. The dog was trying to sing!

Rosa's brother said, "That dog sings! Archie can not learn to sing!"

Just then Mrs. Gates called, "The seven ribbons are lost! Please try to find them and bring them to me. I lost all seven of them during the pet show."

Just then Rosa tripped. She knocked into the table. Archie hopped down from the table and into a box. It was the box with the seven ribbons.

Rosa gave the box to Mrs. Gates. The ribbons had Archie's tracks on them.

Mrs. Gates put a ribbon on Archie and said, "This is what Archie does well! He finds things that are lost! Archie wins for finding the ribbons!"

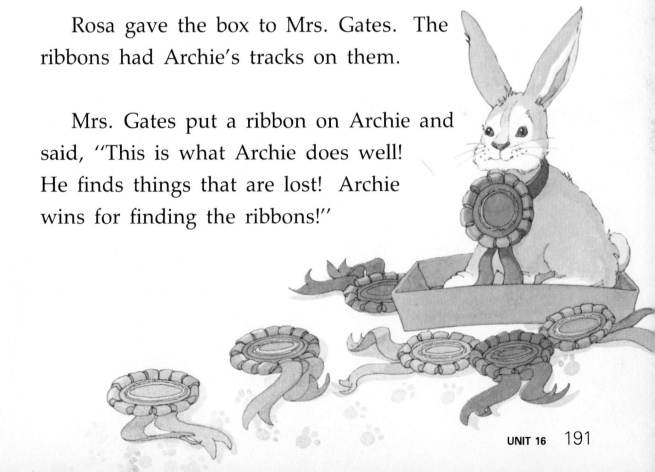

Pet Show

by Arthur Guiterman

We had a pet show out on our lawn,

And one little girl brought a real, live
fawn,

And one small boy dragged a black bull
calf,

Another had a raccoon that would make
you laugh.

There were twelve nice dogs with well
groomed coats,

Twenty-two kittens with bows at their
throats,

A turtle and a frog from down by the
lake,

A goldfish, a pony, and a garter snake,

They were shown by children of various
sizes

Who all had ice cream and all won
prizes.

See a Magic Show

The audience has come to see a magic show. During the show, they see some magic tricks. They seem to like the magic show.

Will the Show Go On?

Mary brought her case of magic tricks into the room. She started to take several things out of the case. Mary's little sister, Karla, wanted to see what was in the case.

Karla said, "Look at all these wonderful things! Will you show me how to do a magic trick with this wand?"

Mary said, "Not now. My audience will be here soon. I must get these things out of the case for my magic show. I'll need my clear magic wand and this blanket for a trick. Please don't play with these things before my show."

But Karla wanted to do a magic trick. As soon as Mary left the room, Karla picked up the clear magic wand to hold it. She waved the wand. She went spinning around and said several things that seemed like magic. And just like that, Karla dropped the wand. It broke!

Karla wondered what to do about the wand she broke. How would Mary put on her magic show? Karla started to make a new wand out of a stick. As she made it, she wondered if it would work.

When it was time for Mary's magic show to start, the audience sat down on a blanket. Mary's case of magic things was on the table. Mary was holding the new magic wand. She wondered where her clear wand was, but she had no time to find out. She had to start the show.

Mary said, "Hello, one and all! I'll
start my magic show by doing a trick
with these spoons. First, audience,
tell me how many spoons you see."

A boy sitting on the blanket called,
"I see nine spoons."

Mary said, "Very good. Now I'll make
these nine spoons turn into ten. Nine
spoons, nine spoons, now make ten!"

Mary stirred her wand around several times. She moved the spoons on the table. With her hand, Mary made the spoons read "TEN."

The audience liked the trick. Karla was happy that the new wand worked, even if it was not clear like the one she broke. After the show, she would tell Mary that she broke the clear wand.

A Little Magic

As the show went on, Mary said, "Now I'll try to find one of your names in my hat. Please tell me your names. I'll write several of them on these papers."

All ten children that lived on Mary's block called out their names. Mary started writing, but she did not write their names. She put Karla's name on all ten papers. Then she put the ten papers into her black hat. No one in the audience knew what she did.

Mary said, "First I'll stir these names around. I'll stir them around several more times. Then I'll try to find your name, Karla."

Mary said something that seemed like magic. She waved the wand several times. She picked one paper.

"This paper says 'Karla!'" Mary said.

The audience clapped for Mary's good trick. So did Karla!

Mary said, "For my last trick, I'll make all of you in the audience go away. With a stir of the wand I am holding, I'll not see you and you will not see me. One, two, three, you I do not see."

Mary stirred her magic wand around. She picked up a small blanket from her case. She put the blanket on her head.

Under the blanket, Mary said, "Now, I don't see you! Can you see me?"

The audience clapped and said, "No!"

Mary had put on a good magic show.

After the show, Karla talked to Mary.

Karla said, "I wanted to do magic
tricks like you. I played with your
clear magic wand. But then I broke it.
I had to make a new one for your show."

Mary said, "I know you broke it. But
it seems to me that you have already
learned to do a little magic of your
own. You made a magic wand for me!
Next time you can put on a magic show of
your own!"

And, before long, Karla did.

Just for You

Do a magic trick. Before your audience comes, cut a small hole in a little white ball.

Do these things to do the trick:
1. Hold the ball in your left hand to hide it. Hold up some bright ribbon with your right hand. Tell the audience that you will make the ribbon turn into a little ball.

1

2. Stir your magic wand around the ribbon several times. Say something that seems like magic.

3. Push the ribbon into your hand and into the hole in the ball.

4. Hold up the white ball in your hand for everybody to see. The ribbon has seemed to turn into a ball. You did a magic trick! Your audience will clap.

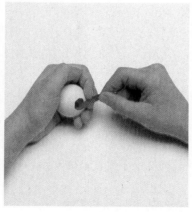

2   3   4

The King's Tree

adapted by Ruth Kaye

Once long ago, a brave and good king lived in a place far away. The king had four, fine boys. He liked spending time with them. During their times together, they would play games. They made music on several of their instruments. But even more than these things, the boys liked to hike with their father.

One winter day, the boys hiked with their father through the snow. They seemed to hike a long way before they saw a big, brown tree. The king wanted to show his boys a tree he liked.

The king said, "This is a wonderful
tree. It is not green like a pine tree,
but I like it. It has a pretty shape."

One of them asked, "What is so good
about this tree? It seems as though it
is made of many spikes. I can not
imagine why you like it, Father."

"You will see," said Father.

Then the king and his boys hiked back
to their house. During their walk, they
did not talk about the tree at all.

The next time the king went hiking with his boys, it was a warm, spring day. During their hike, the five saw a flock of birds fly by in the sky. They hiked by a small lake to see several turtles and ducks.

Then Father led them to see the tree he liked so well. It was white with many blossoms.

The king said, "Look at the wonderful tree now! It is so pretty when it blossoms."

One brother said, "It seems pretty, but the blossoms don't seem to last. Several of these blossoms are already falling to the ground."

The king said, "No, these blossoms don't last long. But some day you will like this tree as well as I do."

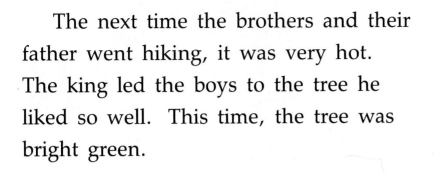

The next time the brothers and their father went hiking, it was very hot. The king led the boys to the tree he liked so well. This time, the tree was bright green.

The king said, "Come and sit under this wonderful tree. It does not seem so hot here, out of the sun. I know you will like the tree now."

The boys sat down with their father.

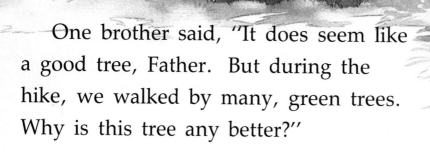

One brother said, "It does seem like a good tree, Father. But during the hike, we walked by many, green trees. Why is this tree any better?"

Father laughed and said, "This tree will give you something that the trees in the woods don't give. In the fall, you will be very happy that I showed you this tree."

During their hike back, the boys talked about what the tree might give them. They wanted fall to come soon.

At last, fall came. The brothers asked their father to take them to the tree he liked so well. They skipped after the king as he led the way. They had not imagined the tree would seem so wonderful. The four brothers saw many bright, red apples on the tree.

As the king and his boys clipped several apples from the tree, the little brother said, "Father, these apples are good. This is a wonderful tree!"

And with that, the king and his four boys ate several apples. They sat and ate under the tree they liked so well.

Books to Read

Clowns by Eugene Baker

What are some of the funny things
that clowns do? Which clown in the book
would you like to be?

Harbor by Donald Crews

What kind of boats are in the water?
Find out what tugs can do.

My Puppy by Mike Thaler

What kind of funny pet does the boy
have for the pet show? What does he
win at the pet show?

Picture Dictionary

dinosaur   dinosaurs
A dinosaur was an animal that lived long ago. Some dinosaurs ate plants.

groundhog   groundhogs
A groundhog lives in a hole in the ground. Groundhogs sleep through the winter.

raccoon   raccoons
A raccoon looks as if it has a black mask. Raccoons like to swim.

zebra   zebras
A zebra is a wild animal. Zebras look like horses with stripes.

Words That Name Things

blanket   **blankets**
A blanket keeps you warm. Some blankets are soft and fluffy.

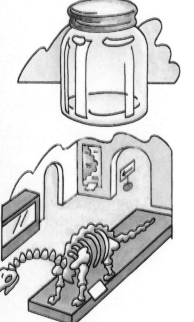

jar   **jars**
A jar holds things. Jars are made of glass.

museum   **museums**
A museum is a place where you can see old things and new things. People go to museums to learn and have fun.

window   **windows**
A window is made of clear glass. We look through windows to see things.

Action Words

follow　　**following**
Follow me to the parade. The dog is
following us.

push　　**pushing**
Pablo will push the box into the room.
He is pushing as hard as he can.

spill　　**spilling**
The paint will spill from the can. It
is spilling on Katy.

swim　　**swimming**
Tina likes to swim. She goes
swimming on a hot day.

Ways To Use Words

glass   glasses

Millie has a glass of milk.

The window is made of glass.

rock   rocks

The boys saw a big rock.

Father rocks the baby.

sign   signs

Sign your name on the line.

Jack reads the sign.

stand   stands

Beth stands up to see how big she is.

Peter buys something to drink at this stand.

Ways To Use Words

track   **tracks**

The train runs on the tracks.

The rabbit makes tracks in the snow.

trip   **trips**

Mrs. Brown might trip on the skate.

Lynn is going on a trip.

tug   **tugs**

The children tug on the rope.

The tug will push the boat through
the water.

wave   **waves**

Carlo waves to his grandma.

The waves rock the boat.

Things I Need To Know

Where you see this sign, you can walk to school. Look for cars before you walk.

Look both ways for a train before you walk near here.

Call these people if you need help.

Call here if you see a fire. The firefighters will come to put out the fire.

Things I Need To Know

Here you can pick out books to read.
What a wonderful place this is!

This is where you go if you are sick.
People will take care of you.

If you don't feel well, look for this
sign. You will get help.

This sign tells you not to go near
a place.

Word List

The words below are listed by unit. Following each word is the page of first appearance of the word.